And Then What Happened, Paul Revere?

by Jean Fritz
Illustrated by Margot Tomes

_____
NAME

What is your definition of a hero? Who are your heroes?

Name Date

Get the Details

Read each main idea from *And Then What Happened, Paul Revere?* Write details that support the main idea.

MAIN IDEA
Paul Revere was a patriot.

_____
_____
_____
_____

MAIN IDEA
Paul Revere had many talents.

_____
_____
_____
_____

2 And Then What Happened, Paul Revere? Details

Name   Date

An Eventful Life

Complete the time line with information you find in *And Then What Happened, Paul Revere?*

January 1, 1735 — Paul Revere is born in Boston, Massachusetts.

1750 — _____

1756 — _____

1765 — _____

December 16, 1773 — _____
1774 — _____
April 18, 1775 — _____

1783 — The Revolutionary War ends.

1818 — _____

How did Paul Revere spend the years after the Revolutionary War?

_____
_____

Sequence   And Then What Happened, Paul Revere? 3

Name   Date

Look for the Clues

Write the meaning of each underlined word.
Use context clues to figure out the meaning.

1. In 1735, Boston passed a law <u>prohibiting</u> people from owning big dogs.

   prohibiting: _____

2. Street <u>vendors</u> sold pills, hair oil, and other goods on the crowded streets.

   vendors: _____

3. Paul rang the church bells whenever a member of the <u>congregation</u> died.

   congregation: _____

4. Paul wrote hurriedly, and his <u>scrawl</u> was sometimes hard to read.

   scrawl: _____

5. Paul slipped by the English <u>transport</u> that lay anchored in the harbor.

   transport: _____

6. Paul galloped through the countryside <u>arousing</u> the sleeping citizens.

   arousing: _____

7. One, then another, and then a <u>succession</u> of shots rang out.

   succession: _____

Find the word *engagements* on page 42 of *And Then What Happened, Paul Revere*? Use context clues to figure out the meaning, and write the meaning below.

engagements: _____

4 And Then What Happened, Paul Revere?   Context clues

Name _____   Date _____

Fact and Opinion

Read each statement below. Decide if it is a fact or an opinion. Then explain how you made your decision.

> A **fact** is a statement based on evidence that can be proved true. An **opinion** is a statement based on a belief or feeling.

Statement	Fact or Opinion?	How I Decided
1. Paul Revere became one of the Sons of Liberty.		
2. Paul Revere took part in the Boston Tea Party.		
3. Paul should not have risked his life and his family's security.		
4. The Boston Tea party was the best way to protest English taxes.		
5. Paul Revere probably enjoyed the excitement and danger of the Boston Tea Party.		

Write another fact and another opinion about Paul Revere.

Fact: _____

Opinion: _____

Fact/opinion

And Then What Happened, Paul Revere?

Name   Date

Stop the Presses!

The year is 1775. You are a news reporter for the *Liberty Press*, a colonial newspaper. Write a news article about Paul Revere's ride. Be sure your article answers these questions: Who? What? Where? When? Why? and How?

Wednesday, April 19, 1775

Liberty Press

Write your headline here.

By: _____

Write your name here.

And Then What Happened, Paul Revere?   *Informative writing*

Map Paul Revere's Ride

The map shows Massachusetts in 1775. Follow the directions below to complete the map.

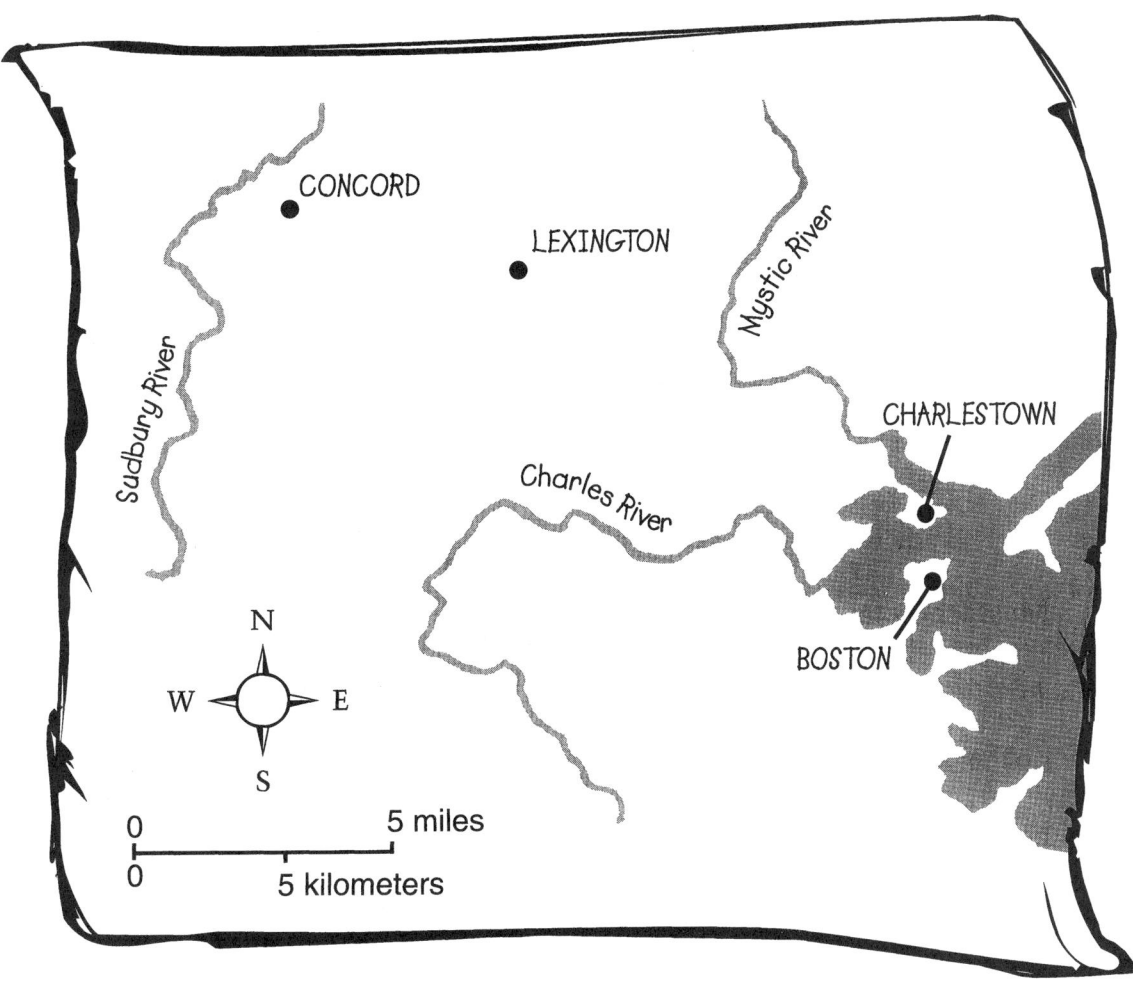

1. Write START at the town where Paul Revere began his ride on April 18.

2. Use a colored pencil to trace the route of the ride.

3. British troops captured Paul Revere about two miles west of Lexington. Draw an ✘ to show where Paul was captured.

4. Draw a 🧰 at the town where John Hancock and Samuel Adams were staying.

5. Draw a ✸ at the town where the British and Americans began fighting.

Graphic aids   And Then What Happened, Paul Revere?

Comma Sense

The summary below of Paul Revere's early life is missing some necessary commas. Use the proofreading mark to show where commas are needed. The first one has been done for you.

Proofreading Marks

Symbol	Meaning
	add a comma

Paul Revere's Early Years
by Lynn Applegate

Paul Revere was born on January 1, 1735 in Boston Massachusetts. Paul's father a goldsmith and silversmith died when Paul was fifteen years old, and Paul took over the family business. He made bracelets pitchers, and other things and he took a second job ringing bells at Christ Church a famous church in the city. Paul was busy but he wanted even more to do. When he was twenty-one years old he went off to fight in the French and Indian War. Paul didn't get to fight any French or Indians but he did swat lots of flies. After Paul returned home, he married Sarah Orne and began a family.

Name _____ Date _____

Final Thoughts

Write a brief summary of *And Then What Happened, Paul Revere?* and give your opinion of it. Be sure to explain why you did or did not like the book.

Title: _____

Author: _____

Illustrator: _____

Summary: _____

_____

_____

_____

_____

_____

My Opinion: _____

_____

_____

Which of your friends do you think would enjoy *And Then What Happened, Paul Revere?* Why?

_____

_____

Evaluate

And Then What Happened, Paul Revere? **9**

Name   Date

Sometimes Things Go Poorly

Things did not always go well for Paul Revere. In the chart below, describe four problems Paul encountered and his solutions.

What do you think was the most serious problem Paul Revere faced? Why?

_____
_____
_____

10 And Then What Happened, Paul Revere?   *Problem/solution*

Name Date

Possessive Power

Read each sentence. Change the underlined part of the sentence to the possessive form, and rewrite the sentence on the line. The first one has been done for you.

1. The hippopotamus teeth of Paul Revere were popular.
   Paul Revere's hippopotamus teeth were popular.

2. The anger of the Patriots was directed at King George.
   _____

3. The disguises of the men fooled the sentries.
   _____

4. The petticoat that belonged to the lady flew out the window.
   _____

5. The plans of the officers were overheard.
   _____

6. The trunk that belonged to John Hancock had been saved.
   _____

7. The route of the riders took them through enemy lines.
   _____

8. Paul told his story again and again at the request of his grandchildren.
   _____

Possessives And Then What Happened, Paul Revere?

Name   Date

Design a Stamp

Design a stamp in honor of Paul Revere. In your design, include a phrase that describes the most important thing about Paul Revere's life. Also, include a drawing.

Explain your stamp design. Tell what your phrase and drawing reveal about Paul Revere.

_____

_____

And Then What Happened, Paul Revere?   *Make judgments*

Name _____   Date _____

Suffix Search

Look at the words in the chart. Circle each base word and underline the suffix. Then write the meaning of the base word and the word with the suffix.

Word	Base Word Means	Suffix Means	Word With Suffix Means
excitement		the condition of	
careful		full of	
orderly		in a certain way	
wooden		made of	
leader		a person who	

Find three other words in *And Then What Happened, Paul Revere?* with the suffix *-er*. Write the words on the lines below.

_____ _____ _____

Suffixes

And Then What Happened, Paul Revere? **13**

Name   Date

A Man of Many Qualities

Complete the web. Write four other adjectives that describe Paul Revere.

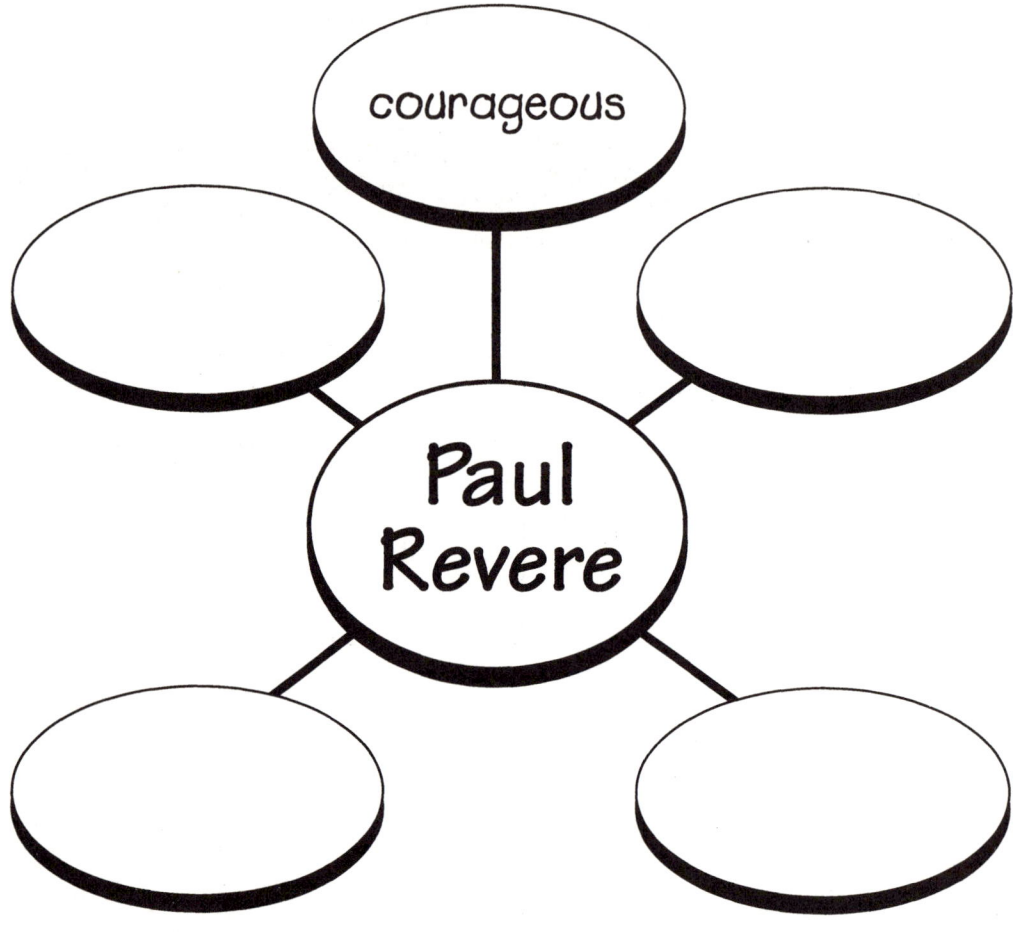

Use the adjectives in the web to write a description of Paul Revere or a poem about him.

_____
_____
_____
_____
_____
_____

And Then What Happened, Paul Revere?   *Descriptive writing*

Quite Puzzling

Use the words in the box from *And Then What Happened, Paul Revere?* to complete the puzzle.

> reinforce   spectacles   retreat   shilling   route
> lampblack   patriot   militia   doodling   foundry

Across

1. an emergency military group
6. a person who loves his or her country
7. to strengthen
8. an English coin
9. to withdraw during an attack

Down

2. fine black soot
3. a factory where metal is cast
4. scribbling aimlessly
5. eyeglasses
7. a course or way

16 And Then What Happened, Paul Revere? Make-Your-Own-Activity Page